Wicked Good Pancakes

Insanely Delicious Savory and Sweet Pancake Recipes

Louise Davidson

ISBN 9798455325113

Printed in the United States

www.TheCookbookPublisher.com

CONTENTS

INTRODUCTION

You might consider pancakes to be an American classic, but pancakes have been around for centuries – even the Greeks and Romans ate them! They're such an easy and versatile food that nearly every culture has its own version.

Every child's dream is to have a plate full of pancakes topped with whipped cream and Nutella. Pancakes are great to have on a cozy winter day, a sunny day on your vacation, or anytime you crave something sweet and delicious but also easy to put together. One of the best things about pancakes is that many recipes allow you to make the batter in five minutes by mixing the dry and wet ingredients.

To celebrate pancakes, we're excited to share this collection of recipes that has something for everyone. The kids love our Brownie Batter Pancakes – and try our Funfetti Buttermilk Pancakes for the birthday boy or girl! Adults and kids alike love our genius Pineapple Upside Down Pancakes. Want crepes instead? We have them, too!

Did you know that pancakes (and crepes) can also be a meal? Our favorites are the Cream Cheese and Herbs Pancakes, but for a more satisfying meal, try the Creamy Chicken and Mushroom Crespelles.

There are things to keep in mind while cooking perfect pancakes. You need to blend the dry ingredients first and then whisk in the wet ingredients – but don't mix too much! The more you mix, the more gluten is activated, resulting in a chewy end result. For pancakes and crepes, we want a more delicate texture, so we take a light hand with the spoon (some lumps are fine).

Pancakes freeze well for up to two months. All you have to do is reheat them in the oven or use a microwave to warm them up. Then you can serve them with your favorite spread, topping, or filling.

Are you ready to join our 50 flavor pancake journey? We're excited for you to get started, so let's find out what your favorites are!

SWEET PANCAKES

Best-Ever Pancakes

For a classic recipe (or a base for your own creation) try this simple and versatile recipe. You won't be disappointed!

Serves 4-6 | Prep. time 10 minutes | Cooking time 10 minutes

Ingredients
1½ cups all-purpose flour
1 teaspoon baking powder
1 teaspoon kosher salt
1 tablespoon granulated sugar
1 large egg, separated
1 teaspoon pure vanilla extract
1⅓ cups milk
2 tablespoons melted butter, plus more for cooking
Maple syrup, for serving

Directions
1. Mix flour, baking powder, salt, and sugar in a large bowl.
2. In a medium bowl, whisk to combine the egg yolk, vanilla, milk, and melted butter. Fold dry ingredients into wet ingredients until just combined.
3. In another medium bowl, using a hand mixer, beat the egg white until stiff peaks form. Fold the egg white into the batter gently with a rubber spatula until just combined.
4. In a large frying pan over medium heat, melt 1 tablespoon butter.
5. Pour about ¼ cup pancake batter into the pan. When little bubbles appear, about 1 to 2 minutes, flip and continue cooking until both sides are lightly golden. Repeat until done. Serve with maple syrup.

Nutrition (per serving)
Calories 236, fat 7 g, carbs 34 g, sugar 5 g,
Protein 7 g, sodium 544 mg

Fluffy Vegan Pancakes

This recipe is a simple and tasty vegan way to serve up a delicious breakfast or brunch. The coconut flavor is very subtle.

Serves 4 | Prep. time 10 minutes | Cooking time 15 minutes

Ingredients
1 cup all-purpose flour
1 tablespoon granulated sugar
1 tablespoon baking powder
¼ teaspoon salt
1 cup almond milk (or any other non-dairy milk)
2 tablespoons coconut oil, melted
Vegetable or coconut oil, for frying
Maple syrup, for serving
Fresh fruit or preserves, for serving (optional)

Directions
1. In a large bowl, whisk together the flour, granulated sugar, baking powder, and salt.
2. Add almond milk and coconut oil and mix until smooth.
3. In a large skillet over medium-low heat, heat a little oil for frying.
4. Using a ¼ cup measure, pour batter into the pan. Cook for 2 to 3 minutes, and flip when you see bubbles forming in the middle of the pancakes. Cook 2 to 3 minutes more on the opposite side, until golden brown in color. (If making a double batch, preheat the oven to 200°F and place the prepared pancakes in a covered dish in the oven to keep them warm.)
5. When all the batter has been used, serve with maple syrup and fruit toppings of your choice.

Nutrition (per serving)
Calories 275, fat 14 g, carbs 29 g, sugar 5 g,
Protein 6 g, sodium 139 mg

Brownie Batter Pancakes

In the mood for chocolate? No worries – we have you covered with these delicious pancakes. You can serve them for breakfast or dessert.

Serves 4 | Prep. time 25 minutes | Cooking time 25 minutes

Ingredients
1 cup all-purpose flour
1¼ cups brownie mix
1 teaspoon baking powder
1 teaspoon baking soda
½ teaspoon salt
2 large eggs
1 cup whole milk
1 teaspoon vanilla extract
½ cup chocolate chips
Cooking spray
Rainbow sprinkles, for serving (optional)
Chocolate syrup, for serving (optional)

Directions
1. In a large bowl, whisk together the flour, brownie mix, baking powder, baking soda, and salt until evenly combined.
2. Beat in the eggs, whole milk, and vanilla. Fold in chocolate chips.
3. Heat a large nonstick pan over medium heat. Lightly coat the pan with cooking spray, then spoon about ¼ cup pancake batter into the pan.
4. When little bubbles appear and start to pop, flip and cook for another 1–2 minutes.
5. Drizzle with chocolate syrup and top with sprinkles, if desired.

Nutrition (per serving)
Calories 386, fat 14 g, carbs 29 g, sugar 18 g,
Protein 15 g, sodium 553 mg

Cream Cheese Pancakes

Rich and comforting, these pancakes are a must-try!

Serves 4–6 | Prep. time 15 minutes | Cooking time 15 minutes

Ingredients
3 ounces cream cheese, softened to room temperature
2 tablespoons sugar
3 large eggs, at room temperature
1 teaspoon pure vanilla extract
Pinch of kosher salt
Butter, for frying
Sliced strawberries, for garnish
Powdered sugar, for garnish
Honey, for serving

Directions
1. In a large bowl, using a hand mixer, beat the cream cheese and sugar until smooth.
2. Add the eggs, vanilla extract, and salt. Beat until well combined.
3. In a large skillet over medium heat, melt a little butter.
4. Pour about ¼ cup of batter into the pan and cook until golden, about 2 minutes. Flip and cook for one more minute.
5. Serve the finished cream cheese pancakes with fresh strawberries and a dusting of powdered sugar.
6. Drizzle with honey, if desired.

Nutrition (per serving)
Calories 123, fat 8 g, carbs 5 g, sugar 5 g,
Protein 5 g, sodium 123 mg

Sweet Potato Pancakes

Here's a great way to use the leftover sweet potatoes from last night's roast dinner. With butter, pecans, and a blend of warming spices, everyone will love these wonderful pancakes.

Serves 8 | Prep. time 25 minutes | Cooking time 45 minutes

Ingredients
1¾ cups all-purpose flour
2 teaspoons baking powder
½ teaspoon baking soda
2 tablespoons light brown sugar
Pinch of salt
1 teaspoon cinnamon
¼ teaspoon ground nutmeg
¼ teaspoon ground ginger
1¾ cups buttermilk
2 small sweet potatoes, roasted and puréed until smooth (about ¾ cup)
2 large eggs, room temperature
1 teaspoon vanilla extract
Butter, for cooking and serving
½ cup toasted pecans, for serving
Maple syrup, for serving

Directions
1. In a large bowl, whisk together the dry ingredients - flour, baking powder, baking soda, brown sugar, salt, cinnamon, nutmeg, and ginger.
2. In a separate bowl, whisk together buttermilk and sweet potato puree, then add eggs and vanilla. Stir until combined.
3. Add wet ingredients to dry ingredients and stir with a wooden spoon until just combined and mixed through.
4. Melt butter in a large nonstick skillet or griddle over medium heat. When butter is foamy, reduce heat to medium-low and scoop with a measuring ½ cup from the pancake batter and dollop it into a skillet.
5. Cook until bubbles start to form in the batter and the pancake is golden underneath, about 3 minutes, then flip

and cook the other side until golden. It will take another 3 minutes.
6. Repeat with the remaining batter.
7. Serve with more butter, toasted pecans, and maple syrup.

Nutrition (per serving)
Calories 352, fat 10 g, carbs 29 g, sugar 15 g,
Protein 16 g, sodium 439 mg

Coconut Oat Pancakes (Gluten-Free)

These wholesome and filling pancakes are suitable for people following a gluten-free diet. Be sure to leave time for the oats to soak.

Serves 4 | Prep. time 20 minutes
Soaking time 2 hours | Cooking time 15 minutes

Ingredients
1½ cups gluten-free oats
½ cup coconut flakes
1 (14-ounce) can coconut milk
1 teaspoon vanilla extract
⅓ cup gluten-free all-purpose flour or oat flour
3 large eggs, room temperature
¼ cup maple syrup
¼ cup coconut oil, melted
1 teaspoon baking powder
Pinch of salt

Optional toppings
Jam
Fruit
Yogurt
Maple syrup

Directions
1. In a large mixing bowl, combine the oats, coconut, coconut milk, and vanilla extract. Allow to soak for at least 2 hours or overnight.
2. In a high-speed blender, combine the flour, eggs, maple syrup, coconut oil, baking powder, and salt. Pour in the soaked oats and coconut and pulse until homogeneous mixture forms.
3. Heat a nonstick frying pan over medium heat.
4. Grease your pan with butter and cook the pancakes until the edges start to bubble and look cooked, 4–5 minutes per side.
5. Serve with fresh jam, fruit, yogurt, or maple syrup.

Nutrition (per serving)
Calories 477, fat 28 g, carbs 47 g, sugar 16 g,
Protein 10 g, sodium 195 mg

Tiramisu Pancakes

If you love tiramisu (and who doesn't?) step right up – we have a recipe for you! Surprise your loved ones with these decadent pancakes soon.

Serves 4 | Prep. time 20 minutes | Cooking time 20 minutes

Ingredients
1 cup all-purpose flour
1 teaspoon baking powder
½ teaspoon baking soda
1 tablespoon sugar
Pinch of salt
¾ cup buttermilk
1 large egg, room temperature
2 tablespoons melted butter
½ teaspoon pure vanilla extract
Butter for frying

For the topping
½ cup heavy whipping cream
1 tablespoon powdered sugar
¼ cup mascarpone cheese, room temperature
½ cup strong coffee, brewed
2 tablespoons cocoa powder

Directions
1. In a large mixing bowl, whisk together the flour, baking powder, baking soda, sugar, and salt until combined.
2. Add the buttermilk, egg, butter, and vanilla into the dry ingredients and whisk until smooth and mixed through.
3. Melt some butter in a nonstick pan and add ¼ cup of the pancake mixture and cook until golden brown on each side.
4. In the bowl of an electric mixer, combine the whipping cream and powdered sugar and whip until stiff peaks form.
5. Gently add the mascarpone into the whipping cream and beat until just combined.
6. To assemble the pancakes, put the coffee in a shallow dish. Briefly dip a pancake into the coffee, plate it, and

spread a little of the cream mixture on top. Sift a thin layer of cocoa powder over the cream.

7. Continue to stack until all the pancakes are used. The top layer should be mascarpone cream dusted with cocoa powder.

Nutrition (per serving)

Calories 475, fat 24 g, carbs 49 g, sugar 35 g, Protein 18 g, sodium 69 mg

French Toast Pancakes

Can't choose between French toast and pancakes? We've got you covered!

Serves 4 | Prep. time 10 minutes | Cooking time 20 minutes

Ingredients
For the pancakes
1 cup all-purpose flour
2 tablespoons sugar
1 teaspoon cinnamon
1 teaspoon baking soda
½ teaspoon baking powder
Pinch of salt
1 cup buttermilk
1 large egg, room temperature
2 tablespoons vegetable oil
1 teaspoon vanilla extract
Butter for frying

For making the French toast
2 large eggs, room temperature
½ cup milk
¼ teaspoon ground cinnamon
Butter for frying

Maple syrup, whipped cream, and fruit for serving (optional)

Directions
1. In a medium bowl combine the flour, sugar, cinnamon, baking soda, baking powder, and salt.
2. In another bowl, mix the buttermilk, egg, vegetable oil, and vanilla extract.
3. Mix the wet ingredients into the dry just until combined.
4. Warm a nonstick frying pan over medium heat and brush with a little butter.
5. Using a ¼ cup measure, spoon the pancake mixture into the warm pan.
6. Cook until the pancakes are golden brown on the bottom and then flip them over to cook on the other side. Repeat this for the remaining pancake mixture.

7. Let the pancakes cool down a little bit.
8. Meanwhile, beat the eggs, milk, and cinnamon in another bowl.
9. Deep each pancake in the egg mixture for 15 seconds on each side.
10. Melt some butter on the griddle and cook the pancakes for 2 more minutes.
11. Serve with maple syrup, whipped cream, or fresh fruit, and enjoy.

Nutrition (per serving)
Calories 375, fat 18 g, carbs 40 g, sugar 25 g,
Protein 16 g, sodium 425 mg

Maple Bar Pancakes

These pancakes are reminiscent of the maple squares of your childhood.

Serves 4 | Prep. time 10 minutes | Cooking time 10 minutes

Ingredients

For pancakes
2 cups all-purpose flour
Pinch of salt
2 teaspoons baking powder
1 teaspoon baking soda
½ teaspoon cinnamon
2 tablespoons sugar
2 large eggs room temperature
2 cups of buttermilk
2 tablespoons butter, melted

Maple glaze
¼ cup butter, melted
1½ cups powdered sugar
¼ cup whole milk
1 teaspoon maple extract
1 teaspoon vanilla extract

Directions

1. In a medium bowl, mix the flour, salt, baking powder, baking soda, cinnamon, and granulated sugar.
2. In another bowl, whisk the eggs with the buttermilk and melted butter.
3. Pour the wet ingredients into the dry, and stir until just combined.
4. Preheat a griddle to medium heat and brush with a little bit of oil to prevent your pancakes from sticking.
5. Using a ⅓ cup measure, scoop the mixture onto the griddle and cook until bubbles begin to form. Flip and cook until golden brown on each side.
6. To make the glaze, combine the ingredients and mix well.
7. When the pancakes have cooled slightly, serve with a generous smear of glaze on top.

Nutrition (per serving)
Calories 299, fat 12 g, carbs 35 g, sugar 15 g,
Protein 12 g, sodium 112 mg

Carrot Cake Pancakes

Enjoy the classic flavor of carrot cake in pancake form!

Serves 4 | Prep. time 10 minutes | Cooking time 10 minutes

Ingredients

For the pancakes

1 cup all-purpose flour
1 teaspoon baking powder
½ teaspoon baking soda
Pinch of salt
1 teaspoon ground cinnamon
1 teaspoon ground nutmeg
1 teaspoon ground ginger
1 large egg, room temperature
2 tablespoons brown sugar
1 cup whole milk
1 teaspoon pure vanilla extract
2 cups carrots, grated

For the glaze

4 ounces cream cheese
¼ cup powdered sugar
2 tablespoons milk
1 teaspoon vanilla

Directions

1. In one large bowl, stir together the flour, baking powder, baking soda, salt, cinnamon, ginger, and nutmeg.
2. In another bowl, mix the egg, brown sugar, whole milk, vanilla, and grated carrots.
3. Add the wet ingredients to the dry ingredients and fold them in until combined.
4. Warm a nonstick frying pan over medium heat and brush with a little bit of butter or oil.
5. Using a ¼ cup measure, scoop out the pancake mixture and dollop it into the warm pan.
6. Cook until bubbles begin to form, and then flip and cook until golden brown and cooked through.

7. To make the glaze, in another bowl, beat the cream cheese with the powdered sugar, milk, and vanilla extract.
8. Drizzle over the pancakes to serve and enjoy.

Nutrition (per serving)
Calories 345, fat 12 g, carbs 38 g, sugar 25 g,
Protein 11 g, sodium 449 mg

Japanese Soufflé Pancakes

These pancakes have a wonderful spongy cake texture. Give them a try!

Serves 6–8 | Prep. time 20 minutes | Cooking time 35 minutes

Ingredients
4 large eggs, room temperature
½ teaspoon lemon juice
Pinch of salt
6 tablespoons granulated sugar, divided
2 large egg yolks, room temperature
2 teaspoons vanilla extract
1 teaspoon baking powder
¼ cup whole milk
6 tablespoons all-purpose flour
2 tablespoons salted butter, melted
Butter, powdered sugar, and fruit for serving (optional)

Directions
1. Combine the egg whites, lemon juice, and salt in the bowl of a stand mixer and whip for about a minute on medium speed until they're foamy.
2. Meanwhile, in a separate bowl, combine the egg yolks with 1 tablespoon of sugar, vanilla, and baking powder. Mix well, and then whisk in the milk and flour.
3. With the mixer running, gradually add the rest of the sugar to the egg whites.
4. Turn the mixer to high and beat until they are stiff and doubled in volume.
5. Carefully add scoops of the egg yolk mixture and gently fold them into the whites until well combined and fluffy.
6. Arrange four 3-inch pastry rings (1½ inch high) in a nonstick skillet and brush with butter. Warm them on low, keeping the lid nearby.
7. Pour a ½ cup of batter into each pastry ring and cover. Cook 3–4 minutes until bubbles form on the surface. Carefully turn them over, cover, and cook another 2–3 minutes.
8. Repeat to make 4 more pancakes.

9. Serve with a dusting of powdered sugar or fruit and jam of your choice.

Nutrition (per serving)
Calories 159, fat 9 g, carbs 28 g, sugar 15 g,
Protein 12 g, sodium 139 mg

Pancake Cereal

What is pancake cereal, you may ask? Let us explain! Pancake cereal is what you get when you make a lot of tiny pancakes and serve them in a bowl with butter and syrup.

Serves 2–4 | Prep. time 10 minutes | Cooking time 15 minutes

Ingredients
1½ cups all-purpose flour
1 teaspoon baking powder
¼ teaspoon baking soda
1 teaspoon kosher salt
1 tablespoon granulated sugar
1 large egg, separated
1 teaspoon pure vanilla extract
1⅓ cups milk
2 tablespoons melted butter, plus more for cooking
Maple syrup, for serving

Directions
1. Mix the flour, baking powder, baking soda, salt, and sugar in a large bowl.
2. In a medium bowl, whisk to combine the egg yolk, vanilla, milk, and melted butter.
3. Fold dry ingredients into wet ingredients until just combined.
4. In another medium bowl, using a hand mixer, beat the egg white until stiff peaks form. Fold the egg white into the batter gently with a rubber spatula until just combined.
5. In a large frying pan over medium heat, melt 1 tablespoon butter. Using a teaspoon, dot the pan with pancake batter, making the pancakes uniform size.
6. When little bubbles appear, about 1 minute, flip and continue cooking until both sides are lightly golden. Repeat with the remaining batter.
7. Serve in a bowl with a pat of butter and maple syrup.

Nutrition (per serving)
Calories 236, fat 7 g, carbs 34 g, sugar 5 g,
Protein 7 g, sodium 544 mg

Instant Pot Giant Pancake

If you don't want to stand in front of a frying pan, toss these ingredients in your Instant Pot and go do something else for a while. You'll come back to a fluffy, delicious pancake for everyone to enjoy.

Serves 8 | Prep. time 10 minutes | Cooking time 45 minutes

Ingredients
2 cups all-purpose flour
1½ cups milk
2 large eggs, room temperature
2 tablespoons granulated sugar
2 teaspoons baking powder
1 teaspoon kosher salt
Cooking spray
1 tablespoon butter, for serving
Maple syrup, for serving

Directions
1. In a large bowl, mix all ingredients together until smooth.
2. Using nonstick cooking spray, generously coat the bottom and sides of a 6-quart Instant Pot.
3. Pour the batter into the pot and seal the lid. Set to low pressure. Cook for 45 minutes.
4. Release the steam and use a toothpick to check that the pancake is cooked in the middle.
5. Use a spatula to remove the pancake from the pot.
6. Serve with butter and maple syrup.

Nutrition (per serving)
Calories 180, fat 4 g, carbs 29 g, sugar 5 g,
Protein 6 g, sodium 342 mg

FRUITY PANCAKES

Blueberry Pancakes

Here's a classic recipe for everyone's first choice of pancake!

Serves 4-6 | Prep. time 10 minutes | Cooking time 10 minutes

Ingredients
1½ cups all-purpose flour
Pinch of salt
1½ teaspoons baking powder
2 tablespoons granulated sugar
2¼ cups buttermilk
1 teaspoon vanilla extract
2 large eggs, room temperature, lightly beaten
2 tablespoons butter, melted
2 cups fresh blueberries
3 tablespoons maple syrup, for serving

Directions
1. In a large mixing bowl mix the flour, salt, and baking powder.
2. Stir in the granulated sugar and mix until combined.
3. In a separate bowl, combine the buttermilk, vanilla extract, and eggs.
4. Mix until combined and stir in the melted butter.
5. Add the wet ingredients to the dry, and stir just to combine.
6. Warm a nonstick frying pan over medium heat and spray it with cooking spray (or brush it with a little bit of butter) to prevent your pancakes from sticking.
7. Add ¼ cup or so of the batter and sprinkle some blueberries on top.
8. Cook for 2–3 minutes (until the edges begin to turn golden) and flip the pancake. Cook 2 more minutes on the other side.
9. Serve your pancakes with fresh blueberries and some maple syrup.

Nutrition (per serving)
Calories 336, fat 8 g, carbs 56 g, sugar 23 g,
Protein 10 g, sodium 211 mg

Spiced Apple Pancakes

The autumn is a great time to enjoy these apple pancakes with their warm, sweet apple topping.

Serves 4–6 | Prep. time 15 minutes | Cooking time 25 minutes

Ingredients
1⅓ cups all-purpose flour
1 teaspoon baking powder
1 teaspoon cinnamon, divided
1 tablespoon granulated sugar
Pinch of salt
2 tablespoons butter
1 large egg, separated
1 teaspoon pure vanilla extract
1¼ cup whole milk
1 large apple, cored and finely chopped

For the topping
2 tablespoons butter
4 large apples, peeled, cored, and finely chopped (about 4 cups)
½ cup brown sugar
½ teaspoon cinnamon
¼ cup water

Butter for frying

Directions
1. In a large mixing bowl, combine the flour, baking powder, cinnamon, granulated sugar, and salt.
2. Melt the butter. In a large bowl, whisk to combine the egg yolk, vanilla, whole milk, and melted butter. Gently fold the dry ingredients into the wet until just until combined, then fold in 1 chopped apple.
3. In another medium bowl, using a hand mixer, beat the egg white until stiff peaks form. Fold the egg white into the batter gently with a rubber spatula until just combined.
4. To make the apple topping, in a small saucepan over medium heat, melt the butter. Add the apples, brown sugar, cinnamon, and water. Cook, stirring occasionally

until the apples have softened and the mixture is yummy for 10–15 minutes.

5. In a large skillet over medium heat, melt a little butter. Pour about ¼ cup of pancake batter into the pan. When little bubbles appear, about 1 to 2 minutes, flip and continue cooking until both sides are lightly golden. Repeat with the remaining batter, adding more butter to the pan as needed.
6. Serve pancakes topped with apple mixture.

Nutrition (per serving)
Calories 356, fat 8 g, carbs 36 g, sugar 20 g,
Protein 12 g, sodium 456 mg

Pineapple Upside-Down Pancakes

We love eating these pineapple upside-down pancakes with their pretty colors and the burst of pineapple flavor. They're also fun to make.

Serves 10 | Prep. time 10 minutes | Cooking time 20 minutes

Ingredients
2 cups Bisquick™
1 cup whole milk
2 large eggs, room temperature
1 teaspoon pure vanilla extract
Butter for frying
10 pineapple rings
10 maraschino cherries (without stems)
⅓ cup packed brown sugar
Whipped cream, for serving
Maple syrup, for serving

Directions
1. In a large bowl, whisk together the Bisquick, whole milk, eggs, and vanilla extract.
2. In a large skillet over medium heat, melt about 1 tablespoon butter.
3. Add a generous ¼ cup of the pancake batter to the skillet and cook for 2 minutes, then add a pineapple ring in the center of the pancake and a cherry in the center of the ring.
4. Sprinkle with a bit of brown sugar. Cook until the edges start to bubble and then about 1 minute more, then flip and reduce heat to medium-low. Cook until golden, approximately 3 more minutes.
5. Repeat with the remaining batter.
6. Serve with whipped cream and maple syrup.

Nutrition (per serving)
Calories 321, fat 18 g, carbs 35 g, sugar 20 g,
Protein 14 g, sodium 439 mg

Banana Walnut Pancakes

Adults and kids alike will love the flavors of banana and walnut in these pancakes, and the nuts give them a very pleasant texture.

Serves 8 | Prep. time 10 minutes | Cooking time 20 minutes

Ingredients
1½ cups all-purpose flour
1 tablespoon baking powder
2 tablespoons packed brown sugar
1 teaspoon kosher salt
¾ cup whole milk
½ cup sour cream
2 large eggs, room temperature
1 teaspoon pure vanilla extract
3 bananas, peeled and diced
3 tablespoons honey
¼ cup walnuts, chopped

Directions
1. In a large bowl, whisk the flour, baking powder, brown sugar, and salt
2. In a separate bowl, whisk the milk and sour cream, then add eggs one at a time, mixing well between each addition. Stir in the vanilla extract.
3. Add wet ingredients to dry ingredients and stir with a wooden spoon until just combined.
4. Using a measuring ¼ cup add dollops from the pancake batter to the warmed skillet or nonstick frying pan over medium heat.
5. Cook your pancakes for about 2 minutes on each side and serve them with sliced bananas, a drizzle of honey, and a sprinkle of chopped walnuts.
6. Enjoy.

Nutrition (per serving)
Calories 253, fat 7 g, carbs 43 g, sugar 19 g,
Protein 6 g, sodium 462 mg

Apple Pancakes with Caramel Apple Syrup

Caramel apples? Yes, please! If you're a fan, then you'll love the apple caramel combination in these pancakes. (And there's no chopping!)

Serves 4 | Prep. time 10 minutes | Cooking time 20 minutes

Ingredients

For the pancakes
1½ cups all-purpose flour
2 tablespoons sugar
2 teaspoons baking powder
1 teaspoon baking soda
Pinch of salt
2 eggs, separated, room temperature
1 cup Greek vanilla yogurt
1 cup apple cider

For the caramel apple syrup
¼ cup butter
¼ cup apple cider
1 cup brown sugar

Directions

1. In a large mixing bowl, mix the flour, sugar, baking powder, baking soda, and salt.
2. Add the egg yolks, Greek vanilla yogurt, and apple cider into the dry ingredients and mix just until combined.
3. In another bowl, beat the egg whites until stiff peaks form and fold them into the pancake mixture.
4. Warm a nonstick frying pan over medium heat and brush with a little bit of butter or vegetable oil.
5. Using a ¼ cup measure, scoop some of the pancake batter and cook your pancakes for about 2–3 minutes on each side. Set them aside.
6. Meanwhile, make the syrup. In a small saucepan over medium, heat the butter and stir in the apple cider.
7. Stir in the brown sugar and cook until bubbly and thick, around 2–3 minutes.

8. Serve the caramel apple syrup on top of the pancakes and enjoy.

Nutrition (per serving)
Calories 325, fat 14 g, carbs 42 g, sugar 25 g,
Protein 13 g, sodium 529 mg

Orange Buttermilk Pancakes

Change up your morning flapjacks with a cheery burst of orange flavor. These are delicious with any kind of sliced fruit.

Serves 6 | Prep. time 15 minutes | Cooking time 30 minutes

Ingredients
2 cups all-purpose flour
Pinch of salt
1½ teaspoons baking powder
½ teaspoon baking soda
¼ cup granulated sugar
3 large eggs, room temperature
¾ cup whole milk
¾ cup orange juice
2 tablespoons orange zest
5 tablespoons butter, melted
1 tablespoon vegetable oil

Directions
1. In a large mixing bowl, combine the flour, salt, baking powder, baking soda, and granulated sugar.
2. In another bowl, beat the eggs and mix in the whole milk, orange juice, and orange zest.
3. Stir in the melted butter and whisk until combined.
4. Add the wet ingredients to the dry ingredients and mix until just combined. Be careful not to overmix the batter.
5. Warm the oil in a nonstick frying pan over medium heat and using a ¼ cup measure, scoop some of the pancake batter and cook until golden brown on each side.
6. Top each pancake on top of another to keep them warm
7. Serve with a dusting of powdered sugar or fruit and jam of your choice.

Nutrition (per serving)
Calories 289, fat 14 g, carbs 29 g, sugar 18 g,
Protein 11 g, sodium 199 mg

Avocado Pancakes

These green pancakes are flavorful and pretty – a perfect choice for St. Patrick's Day!

Serves 4–6 | Prep. time 10 minutes | Cooking time 10 minutes

Ingredients
1½ cups all-purpose flour
Pinch of salt
1½ teaspoons baking soda
1 cup whole milk
2 avocados, mashed
2 tablespoons butter, melted
2 large eggs, room temperature
3 tablespoons cream cheese

Directions
1. In a large mixing bowl, mix the flour, salt, and baking powder.
2. Add the whole milk, mashed avocado, melted butter, and eggs. Mix just to combine.
3. Warm a nonstick frying pan over medium heat and spray it with cooking spray or brush it with a little bit of butter to prevent your pancakes from sticking.
4. Cook for 2–3 minutes and flip to cook the other side.
5. Serve your pancakes with a schmear of cream cheese.

Nutrition (per serving)
Calories 420, fat 26 g, carbs 38 g, sugar 3 g,
Protein 10 g, sodium 521 mg

FUN FLAVORED PANCAKES

Banana Chocolate Chip Pancake for One

Here's a quick breakfast for one, with little effort and no leftovers.

Serves 1 | Prep. time 10 minutes | Cooking time 10 minutes

Ingredients
⅓ cups all-purpose flour
2 teaspoons sugar
½ teaspoon baking powder
¼ teaspoon baking soda
Pinch of salt
2 tablespoons butter, melted
⅓ cup milk
½ teaspoon vanilla extract
1 tablespoon semi-sweet chocolate chips, more if needed
1 banana, sliced
Maple syrup, for serving

Directions
1. Warm a medium nonstick skillet over medium-low heat.
2. In a small mixing bowl, combine the flour, sugar, baking powder, baking soda, and salt.
3. Stir in the melted butter, milk, and vanilla extract.
4. Brush your pan with butter and pour the batter into the pan.
5. Sprinkle chocolate chips and banana slices on top of the batter. Flip the pancake when bubbles start to surface in the center of the pancake, around 3 minutes. Continue cooking until the pancake is cooked through and both sides are golden.
6. Serve with maple syrup.

Nutrition (per serving)
Calories 539, fat 25 g, carbs 72 g, sugar 26 g,
Protein 8 g, sodium 676 mg

Red Velvet Pancakes with Cream Cheese Glaze

Your family's faces will light up when they see these pancakes coming to the table! We like to serve these on Valentine's Day for a special treat.

Serves 8 | Prep. time 15 minutes | Cooking time 30 minutes

Ingredients

<u>For the pancakes</u>
2⅓ cups all-purpose flour (scoop and level to measure)
3 tablespoons cocoa powder
2 teaspoons baking powder
½ teaspoon baking soda
Pinch of salt
2 cups whole milk
2 tablespoons white vinegar
½ cup granulated sugar
2 large eggs, room temperature, lightly beaten
1½ tablespoons red food coloring
2 teaspoons pure vanilla extract
⅓ cup salted butter, melted

<u>For the glaze</u>
6 ounces cream cheese, softened
6 tablespoons butter, softened
2 cups powdered sugar
⅓ cup milk, plus more if desired
½ teaspoon vanilla extract
Pinch of salt

Directions
1. Warm a nonstick frying pan over medium heat.
2. In a large mixing bowl, whisk the flour, cocoa powder, baking powder, baking soda, and salt. Set aside.
3. In a glass, mix the milk with the vinegar. Stir, and pour it into the bowl with the dry ingredients.
4. Stir in the granulated sugar, eggs, red food coloring, vanilla, and melted butter. Mix just until smooth.

5. Spray your frying pan with butter or cooking spray and pour about a ¼ to a ⅓ cup of batter at a time onto the hot pan.
6. Cook until bubbles begin to appear on the surface of the pancakes, then flip and cook the opposite side until the pancake is cooked through.
7. Meanwhile, make the cream cheese glaze. In a mixing bowl, beat the cream cheese and butter until well combined and fluffy.
8. Add the powdered sugar, whole milk, vanilla extract, and salt, and mix until smooth.
9. To serve, top your pancakes with the cream cheese glaze.

Nutrition (per serving)
Calories 410, fat 14 g, carbs 49 g, sugar 25 g,
Protein 16 g, sodium 339 mg

Ricotta Pancakes with Blackberry-Orange Syrup

Tart, sweet, and rich, we bet these pancakes are unlike anything you've tried before.

Serves 4-6 | Prep. time 40 minutes | Cooking time 40 minutes

Ingredients
¾ cup all-purpose flour
¾ cup whole wheat flour
1½ teaspoons baking powder
Pinch of salt
2 tablespoons granulated sugar
2 eggs, room temperature, separated
1½ cups whole milk
½ cup ricotta cheese
Butter for frying

For the topping
1 package frozen blackberries
½ cup granulated sugar
1 teaspoon cornstarch
¼ cup pure maple syrup

Ricotta filling
1 orange
1 teaspoon honey
½ cup ricotta cheese

Directions
1. Prepare the sauce. In a saucepan over medium heat, combine the blackberries, sugar, and cornstarch. Cook until they start to bubble.
2. Reduce the heat to low and stir often until the sauce thickens and becomes syrupy. Remove the pot from the heat and stir in the syrup. Set aside to cool.
3. In a large mixing bowl, combine the flours, baking powder, salt, and sugar.
4. In another bowl, mix the egg yolks, whole milk, and ½ cup ricotta.

5. Add the dry into the wet ingredients and whisk just until combined.
6. Beat the egg white until stiff peaks form and fold them into the batter.
7. Warm a nonstick frying pan over medium heat and brush with butter.
8. Add a ¼ cup of pancake batter to the pan and cook for about 2–3 minutes on each side.
9. Cook the pancakes until they're golden brown then transfer them to a baking sheet covered loosely with foil to keep them warm. Repeat this for the remaining pancake mixture.
10. Zest the orange. Keep the zest aside and cut orange segments for garnish.
11. Stir the honey with the ricotta and orange zest in a small bowl.
12. Serve your pancakes with the blackberry sauce and ricotta filling.

Nutrition (per serving)
Calories 315, fat 12 g, carbs 42 g, sugar 15 g,
Protein 15 g, sodium 426 mg

Walnut and Bananas Foster Pancakes

You won't want to miss this recipe – it pairs a classic pancake with a delicious Bananas Foster topping that everyone will love.

Serves 2 | Prep. time 10 minutes | Cooking time 20 minutes

Ingredients
1 cup all-purpose flour
1 teaspoon granulated sugar
1 teaspoon baking powder
Pinch of salt
3 tablespoon melted butter
2 large eggs, room temperature
1 cup whole milk

For the topping
2 tablespoons butter
⅔ cup brown sugar
1 teaspoon vanilla extract
1 tablespoon whole milk
Pinch of salt
2 bananas, sliced
¼ cup chopped walnuts

Butter for frying

Directions
1. Turn the oven to 200°F (94°C).
2. In a medium bowl, combine the flour, granulated sugar, baking powder, and salt.
3. In a small bowl, whisk the melted butter, eggs, and milk to combine. Add the wet ingredients to the dry and whisk until combined.
4. Brush the pan with butter and let it warm on medium heat.
5. Pour a ¼ cup of batter onto the pan.
6. Cook three pancakes at a time. Once you see tiny bubbles start to form, flip the pancakes and continue

cooking for 1 minute or until golden brown. Place the pancakes in the oven to keep them warm.

7. Once all the pancakes are cooked, wipe the frying pan to clean it.
8. Make the topping. Place the butter in the pan and heat until it begins to bubble. Stir in the brown sugar.
9. Add the vanilla extract and the whole milk slowly, whisking while pouring.
10. The sugar will pop and sizzle. Stir until you have a nice thin caramel.
11. Add the sliced bananas and walnuts and coat with the caramel sauce.
12. Continue cooking for a few minutes until the sauce has thickened slightly and the bananas are soft.
13. Top the pancakes with the Bananas Foster sauce, and serve warm.

Nutrition (per serving)
Calories 325, fat 14 g, carbs 39 g, sugar 15 g,
Protein 16 g, sodium 529 mg

Banana Bread Pancakes with Cream Cheese Glaze

These pancakes are comfort food at their finest, and the large batch makes them perfect for a brunch gathering.

Serves 9 | Prep. time 20 minutes | Cooking time 15 minutes

Ingredients
For the pancakes
2 cups all-purpose flour
1 teaspoon baking powder
½ teaspoon baking soda
½ teaspoon salt
½ teaspoon ground cinnamon
¾ cup buttermilk
¼ cup sour cream
3 tablespoons granulated sugar
3 tablespoons light brown sugar
1½ cups mashed overripe bananas (about 3 bananas)
1 large egg, room temperature
½ teaspoon vanilla extract
¼ cup unsalted butter, melted

Glaze
4 ounces cream cheese softened
¼ cup butter softened
1½ cups powdered sugar
6 tablespoons whole milk (depending on the desired consistency)

Directions
1. Warm a nonstick frying pan over medium heat.
2. In a large mixing bowl, whisk together the flour, baking powder, baking soda, salt, and cinnamon. Set aside.
3. In a separate mixing bowl, whisk together the buttermilk, sour cream, granulated sugar, brown sugar, mashed bananas, egg, vanilla, and melted butter.
4. Pour the buttermilk mixture into the flour mixture and stir just until combined. Be careful not to overmix the batter.

5. Scoop ⅓ cup of the batter and cook your pancakes on medium heat for about 2 minutes.
6. When bubbles start to appear, flip the pancakes and continue cooking for another 2 minutes.
7. To make the glaze, in a medium mixing bowl, beat the cream cheese and butter until well combined and fluffy. (About 2 minutes.)
8. Add the remaining ingredients and mix until smooth.
9. When you're ready to serve the pancakes, top them with some of the cream cheese glaze.

Nutrition (per serving)
Calories 425, fat 14 g, carbs 23 g, sugar 12 g,
Protein 10 g, sodium 529 mg

Funfetti Buttermilk Pancakes

Serve these for birthday breakfasts (we like to make them for sleepover breakfasts) or any time you want to delight the kids. With the flavors of buttermilk, vanilla, and almond, the adults will enjoy them too.

Serves 8 | Prep. time 10 minutes | Cooking time 20 minutes

Ingredients
2¼ cups all-purpose flour
⅓ cup granulated sugar
1¼ teaspoons baking powder
½ teaspoon baking soda
Pinch of salt
2 large eggs, room temperature, beaten
2 cups buttermilk
2 teaspoons vanilla extract
¼ teaspoon almond extract
6 tablespoons butter, melted
⅔ cup rainbow sprinkles

For the icing
½ cup icing sugar, sifted
½ teaspoon pure vanilla extract
2 tablespoons whole milk
Extra rainbow sprinkles for serving

Directions
1. In a large mixing bowl, stir the flour, sugar, baking powder, baking soda, and salt. Mix until combined.
2. In the same bowl, mix in the eggs, buttermilk, vanilla extract, and almond extract.
3. Briefly stir in the melted butter and the rainbow sprinkles. Do not overmix, or the colors of the sprinkles will blend together.
4. Warm a nonstick frying pan over medium heat and brush it with a little bit of butter.
5. Scoop out a ¼ cup of batter for each pancake, and cook the pancakes for about 2 minutes on each side.
6. When the bubbles start to appear on the sides of the pancakes, that means that they are ready to be flipped.

7. To make the icing, in a small mixing bowl mix the icing sugar, vanilla extract, and milk until smooth.
8. Serve your pancakes with a drizzle of the icing and a dusting of extra sprinkles.

Nutrition (per serving)
Calories 275, fat 14 g, carbs 29 g, sugar 5 g,
Protein 6 g, sodium 139 mg

Butterscotch Pancakes

Once you try these unique pancakes, your family will be asking for them every weekend!

Serves 8 | Prep. time 15 minutes | Cooking time 30 minutes

Ingredients
1 cup all-purpose flour
½ cup crushed graham crackers
2 tablespoons granulated sugar
1 teaspoon baking powder
½ teaspoon baking soda
½ teaspoon salt
1 cup buttermilk
1 large egg, room temperature
2 tablespoons butter, melted
½ teaspoon vanilla extract
¼ cup butterscotch chips
¼ cup chocolate chips
Butter for frying

For the marshmallow syrup
1 cup marshmallow fluff
2 tablespoons water

Directions
1. In a medium bowl, whisk together the flour, crushed graham crackers, granulated sugar, baking powder, baking soda, and salt.
2. Mix until combined and stir in the buttermilk, egg, melted butter, and vanilla extract.
3. Stir in the butterscotch and chocolate chips and mix until combined. Let the batter sit for 10 minutes.
4. Meanwhile, make the marshmallow syrup. Add the marshmallow fluff and water to a medium bowl and microwave for 15 seconds. Stir until smooth. For a thinner syrup, stir in additional water.
5. Heat a nonstick frying pan on medium heat and melt some butter.
6. Pour the batter into the skillet using a ¼ cup measure. When bubbles start to form on the edges of the

pancakes, flip and cook for an additional minute or so until the pancake is cooked through. Serve with marshmallow syrup on top.

Nutrition (per serving)
Calories 375, fat 19 g, carbs 34 g, sugar 15 g, Protein 16 g, sodium 439 mg

Snickerdoodle Pancakes

If you love snickerdoodle cookies, you're going to love these pancakes.

Serves 4 | Prep. time 10 minutes | Cooking time 10 minutes

Ingredients
For the pancakes
1 cup all-purpose flour
3 tablespoons of sugar
2 teaspoons of cream of tartar
½ teaspoon baking soda
½ teaspoon of kosher salt
2 teaspoons of cinnamon
¼ teaspoon of freshly grated nutmeg
1 cup sour cream
¼ cup melted butter
1 egg, room temperature
⅓ cup whole milk

For the warm cinnamon and vanilla glaze
1 cup icing sugar
1 teaspoon vanilla extract
1 teaspoon cinnamon
3–4 tablespoons of milk

Directions
1. In a large bowl, stir the dry ingredients: flour, sugar, cream of tartar, baking soda, salt, cinnamon, and nutmeg.
2. Add the sour cream, melted butter, egg, and whole milk. Mix just until combined.
3. Warm a nonstick frying pan over medium heat with a little bit of oil.
4. Use a ¼ cup measure to scoop out the mixture and cook the pancakes for 2–3 minutes.
5. When bubbles begin to form, flip the pancakes and cook until golden brown on the other side.
6. To make the vanilla and cinnamon glaze, place the icing sugar, vanilla, cinnamon, and milk in a small saucepan and cook for about 2 minutes.

7. Drizzle the warm glaze on top of the cooked pancakes and enjoy.

Nutrition (per serving)
Calories 325, fat 11 g, carbs 33 g, sugar 22 g,
Protein 12 g, sodium 225 mg

Peppermint Hot Chocolate Pancakes

Serves 4 | Prep. time 10 minutes | Cooking time 10 minutes

Ingredients

1 cup all-purpose flour
⅓ cup unsweetened cocoa powder
2 tablespoons granulated sugar
½ teaspoon baking soda
Pinch of salt
1 cup whole milk
1 large egg, room temperature
2 tablespoons canola oil
⅛ teaspoon peppermint extract
1 tablespoon butter

For serving
½ cup chocolate sauce
¼ cup chocolate chips
¼ cup mini marshmallows
1 tablespoon crushed peppermint candy

Directions

1. In a large mixing bowl, combine the flour, cocoa powder, sugar, salt, and baking soda.
2. In another mixing bowl, beat together the milk, egg, canola oil, and peppermint extract.
3. Mix the dry ingredients into the wet ingredients and stir until combined.
4. Melt some of the butter in a nonstick pan and use a ¼ cup measure to spoon the pancake mixture into the skillet. Cook until bubbles form, and then flip and cook for 2 minutes on the other side, or until cooked through.
5. Top the pancakes with chocolate sauce, chocolate chips, mini marshmallows, and peppermint candy.

Nutrition (per serving)

Calories 325, fat 10 g, carbs 40 g, sugar 28 g,
Protein 12 g, sodium 129 mg

Pancake Poppers

If you're running short on time or want a portable breakfast, try these baked pancakes.

Serves 6 | Prep. time 10 minutes | Cooking time 10 minutes

Ingredients
1½ cups flour
2 tablespoons granulated sugar
2½ teaspoons baking powder
1 teaspoon baking soda
½ teaspoon salt
¾ cup whole milk
2 tablespoons maple syrup
2 tablespoons butter, melted
1 egg, lightly beaten
1 teaspoon vanilla extract
½ teaspoon ground cinnamon
⅔ cup chocolate chips
Maple syrup, for serving

Directions
1. Preheat the oven to 400°F (204°C). Spray a mini muffin pan with cooking spray.
2. In a large bowl, stir together the flour, granulated sugar, baking powder, baking soda, and salt.
3. Stir in the whole milk, maple syrup, melted butter, egg, vanilla, and cinnamon.
4. Fold in mini chocolate chips until just combined.
5. Divide the batter evenly in the mini muffin cups.
6. Bake for 8–10 minutes. Serve warm or at room temperature with maple syrup.

Nutrition (per serving)
Calories 310, fat 11 g, carbs 46 g, sugar 19 g,
Protein 6 g, sodium 474 mg

Eggnog Pancakes

Serves 4–6 | Prep. time 10 minutes | Cooking time 10 minutes

Ingredients
1½ cups all-purpose flour
3 teaspoons baking powder
1 teaspoon salt
1 tablespoon sugar
½ teaspoons nutmeg
1½ cups eggnog
1 egg, straight from the fridge, beaten
3 tablespoons butter, melted
1 teaspoon vanilla extract

For the topping
2 tablespoons sugar
1 teaspoon cinnamon
Pinch nutmeg

Maple syrup, for serving

Directions
1. In a large mixing bowl, mix the flour, baking powder, salt, sugar, and nutmeg.
2. Add the eggnog, egg, butter, and vanilla, and mix until just combined.
3. In a nonstick (or well-greased) frying pan over medium-low heat, pour a ¼ cup from the pancake batter into the center of the pan.
4. Heat until small bubbles form in the pancake and a lip forms around the edge of the edge. Flip and cook the pancakes until completely done. Repeat until all the batter is gone.
5. In a small bowl, combine the remaining sugar and cinnamon.
6. Sprinkle the top of the pancakes and drizzle with syrup before eating.

Nutrition (per serving)
Calories 275, fat 14 g, carbs 29 g, sugar 5 g,
Protein 6 g, sodium 139 mg

Vegan Banana Chocolate Chip Pancakes

These tasty pancakes are perfect for a vegan diet.

Serves 4 | Prep. time 10 minutes | Cooking time 15 minutes

Ingredients
1 cup all-purpose flour
1 tablespoon granulated sugar
2 teaspoons baking powder
Pinch of salt
2 large bananas, ripe and mashed
1¼ cups almond milk
½ cup vegan chocolate chips
Powdered sugar, maple syrup, and chopped nuts for serving (optional)

Directions
1. In a large mixing bowl, combine the flour, granulated sugar, baking powder, and salt.
2. In another bowl, mix the mashed bananas and almond milk.
3. Add the wet ingredients to the dry ingredients and mix just until combined.
4. Fold in the chocolate chips.
5. Warm the oil in a nonstick frying pan over medium heat and using a ¼ cup measure, scoop some of the pancake batter and cook until golden brown on each side.
6. Serve with a dusting of powdered sugar, maple syrup, or chopped nuts.

Nutrition (per serving)
Calories 473, fat 24 g, carbs 60 g, sugar 24 g,
Protein 7 g, sodium 70 mg

CREPES

Classic Crepes

This easy recipe is very versatile and can be used for any crepe creation. Try some out on your own!

Serves 8 | Prep. time 10 minutes | Cooking time 30 minutes

Ingredients
1⅓ cups all-purpose flour
½ teaspoon baking powder
2 tablespoons granulated sugar
1 egg, room temperature
2 cups whole milk

Directions
1. In a large mixing bowl, whisk together the flour, baking powder, salt, and granulated sugar until well combined.
2. Stir in the egg and whole milk into the batter and mix until everything is combined.
3. Warm a nonstick frying pan over medium heat and brush it with a little bit of oil.
4. Add a small amount of the batter, enough to cover the bottom of the pan, evenly spreading it by swirling the pan in a circular motion.
5. Cook for 2 to 3 minutes and when it appears to be set, flip the crepe to cook on the other side.
6. Repeat this process for the rest of the crepe batter.
7. Serve with syrup, whipped cream, or fruit.

Nutrition (per serving)
Calories 133, fat 2 g, carbs 21 g, sugar 6 g,
Protein 4 g, sodium 34 mg

Strawberry Rhubarb Crepes

This recipe is a wonderful change from the ordinary and perfect for the rhubarb season.

Serves 8 | Prep. time 10 minutes | Cooking time 40 minutes

Ingredients

For the crepes
1 cup all-purpose flour
1 tablespoon granulated sugar
Pinch of salt
2 large eggs, room temperature
1¼ cup milk
3 tablespoons cooking oil
1 teaspoon vanilla extract

Roasted rhubarb and strawberries:
3 ounces rhubarb, diced
1 cup fresh strawberries, hulled and diced
2 tablespoons honey

¾ cup Nutella®

Directions

1. Begin by roasting the rhubarb and strawberries. Preheat the oven to 400°F (204°C) and prepare a baking sheet with a generous coating of cooking spray.
2. In a mixing bowl, combine the fruit and honey. Spread it on the sheet and roast for 12–15 minutes. Place the fruit and any juices in a bowl and set them aside.
3. In a large mixing bowl, mix the dry ingredients: flour, granulated sugar, and salt.
4. In another bowl, beat the eggs and add the milk, vegetable oil, and vanilla.
5. Meanwhile, stir the wet ingredients into the dry and mix until smooth. Let it rest for 30 minutes in the fridge.
6. Warm a nonstick frying pan over medium heat and brush with a little bit of oil.
7. Add a little bit of the crepe batter and spread it thinly over the pan.

8. When the edges begin to lift, flip the crepe to continue the cooking process on the other side.
9. Repeat this process for the rest of the mixture.
10. Spread the Nutella on the crepes and add dollops of the roasted strawberries and rhubarb.

Nutrition (per serving)
Calories 252, fat 14 g, carbs 29 g, sugar 16 g,
Protein 6 g, sodium 139 mg

Crepes with Lemon Curd

Serves 8 | Prep. time 10 minutes | Cooking time 30 minutes

Ingredients
For the crepes
¾ cup all-purpose flour
Pinch of salt
2 large eggs, room temperature
1¼ cup whole milk
¼ cup butter, melted

For the lemon curd
¾ cup granulated sugar
2 large eggs, room temperature
2 egg yolks, room temperature
⅓ cup butter, softened
Zest and juice of 2 whole lemons

Directions
1. In a large mixing bowl, combine the flour, salt, eggs, whole milk, and melted butter. Mix until smooth.
2. Warm a nonstick frying pan over medium heat and brush with a little bit of butter or vegetable oil.
3. Pour some of the crepe batter into the hot pan and swirl it around to spread a thin layer. Cook for about 2–3 minutes on each side.
4. Repeat this process for the rest of the crepe batter.
5. To make the lemon curd, place the granulated sugar, eggs, egg yolks, and butter into a heatproof mixing bowl over a pot with simmering water.
6. With a wire whisk, stir until everything is combined and warm. Stir in the lemon zest and lemon juice and cook for 7–10 minutes, until thickened.
7. Serve your crepes with lemon curd.

Nutrition (per serving)
Calories 275, fat 14 g, carbs 29 g, sugar 5 g,
Protein 6 g, sodium 139 mg

Bananas Foster Nutella Crepes

The addition of coffee liqueur makes these crepes extra rich and decadent.

Serves 8 | Prep. time 10 minutes | Cooking time 20 minutes

Ingredients
1 cup all-purpose flour
2 large eggs, room temperature
¾ cup whole milk
½ cup water
2 tablespoons butter
3 bananas, diced
2 tablespoons brown sugar
2 tablespoons Kahlúa®
1 cup Nutella®
Mini chocolate chips

Directions
1. In a large mixing bowl, combine the flour, eggs, whole milk, and water. Mix just until combined.
2. Warm some oil in a nonstick frying pan over medium heat.
3. Pour some of the crepe batter into the skillet and swirl the whole pan in a circular motion to make a thin crepe.
4. Cook for 1–2 minutes and flip to cook the other side.
5. Repeat this process with the rest of the mixture.
6. In a small saucepan over medium heat, melt the butter and add the bananas.
7. Stir in the brown sugar and Kahlúa and cook for 1 more minute.
8. Spread some Nutella on each crepe, add some of the cooked bananas and sauce, and fold the whole crepe together.
9. Top each crepe with chocolate chips and some more Nutella on top.

Nutrition (per serving)
Calories 452, fat 13 g, carbs 42 g, sugar 23 g,
Protein 5 g, sodium 60 mg

Breton Crepes

These crepes are not your everyday ham and cheese. Make them soon, and you'll see what we mean!

Serves 6 | Prep. time 10 minutes
Refrigeration time 2 hours | Cooking time 25 minutes

Ingredients
2 cups buckwheat flour
1 large egg, room temperature
¼ cup melted butter
¼ cup water
Pinch of salt
3 ounces ham slices
2 cups grated Gruyere cheese

Directions
1. In a large mixing bowl, combine the flour, egg, melted butter, water, and salt. Mix until combined.
2. Let the mixture sit in the fridge for 2 hours.
3. Warm some oil in a nonstick frying pan over medium heat.
4. Pour some of the crepe batter and swirl the pan in a circular motion to make thin crepes.
5. Cook for 1-2 minutes and flip to cook the other side.
6. After the crepe is flipped, top with ham and some grated cheese. After 1-2 more minutes, fold the edges toward the center so the cheese is showing.
7. Repeat this process with the rest of the mixture.

Nutrition (per serving)
Calories 389, fat 23 g, carbs 29 g, sugar 5 g,
Protein 6 g, sodium 139 mg

SAVORY PANCAKES AND CREPES

Creamy Chicken Spinach and Pancetta Pancakes

If you love chicken and pancetta, here is a lunch option you'll come back to time and again.

Serves 6 | Prep. time 10 minutes | Cooking time 25 minutes

Ingredients
1 cup all-purpose flour
1 teaspoon baking powder
½ teaspoon baking soda
1 tablespoon granulated sugar
Pinch of salt
¾ cup buttermilk
2 tablespoons butter, melted
1 large egg, room temperature
1 tablespoon olive oil
1 onion, diced
3 ounces pancetta or streaky bacon, diced
7 ounces mushrooms, diced
2 cups shredded chicken, cooked
1½ cups gravy
1½ cups creme fraiche
3 cups baby spinach

Directions
1. In a large mixing bowl, whisk together the flour, baking powder, baking soda, salt, and sugar.
2. In the same bowl, stir in the buttermilk, butter, and egg. Mix until smooth.
3. Warm some oil in a nonstick frying pan over medium heat and using a ¼ cup measure, scoop some of the pancake batter and cook for 2–3 minutes on each side.

4. In a separate pan, warm the olive oil and cook the diced onion and pancetta for 2–3 minutes.
5. Stir in the mushrooms and shredded chicken and cook for 2–3 more minutes.
6. Pour in the gravy, creme fraiche, and spinach and cook to heat through and so the spinach is wilted.
7. Top the pancakes with the creamy chicken mixture and serve warm.

Nutrition (per serving)
Calories 675, fat 20 g, carbs 36 g, sugar 2 g,
Protein 12 g, sodium 1125 mg

Brussels Sprouts Pancakes with Smoked Salmon

Surprise your brunch guests with this restaurant-quality entrée!

Serves 4 | Prep. time 20 minutes | Cooking time 15 minutes

Ingredients
¾ cup all-purpose flour
1 teaspoon baking powder
¼ teaspoon paprika
3 large eggs, room temperature, beaten
¾ cup whole milk
10 ounces Brussel sprouts, shredded
Grated zest of half a lemon
6 tablespoons creme fraiche
2 teaspoons Dijon mustard
Juice of half a lemon
Salt and pepper to taste
8 thin slices smoked salmon
Oil for frying

Directions
1. In a large mixing bowl, whisk together the flour, baking powder, and paprika. Stir in the eggs and milk. Mix until combined
2. Stir in the Brussels sprouts and the lemon zest. Mix just until combined.
3. Warm some oil in a nonstick frying pan over medium heat and cook the pancakes for 2–3 minutes on each side.
4. Repeat with the rest of the pancake batter.
5. Mix the creme fraiche with mustard and lemon juice in a small bowl. Season with salt and pepper to taste.
6. Top each pancake with the creme fraiche mixture and slices of salmon.

Nutrition (per serving)
Calories 281, fat 14 g, carbs 29 g, sugar 5 g,
Protein 6 g, sodium 139 mg

Dhal Chilla Pancakes

These light pancakes are a favorite Indian dish and are very flavorful and healthy. They are often used as a side dish and may come with many kinds of dips and fillings.

Serves 4 | Prep. time 10 minutes + overnight soaking time Cooking time 15 minutes

Ingredients
1 cup yellow lentils, rinsed and soaked overnight
1 inch fresh ginger, finely grated
1 small green chili, minced
2 tablespoons fresh cilantro, chopped
Pinch of salt
¼ cup semolina
Oil for frying

Directions
1. After soaking the lentils overnight, drain them well and place them in a blender with the other ingredients. Process just until smooth, and add water to achieve a consistency that can be poured.
2. In a thick-bottomed skillet, heat a few drops of oil until hot.
3. Spoon some batter into the pan and use the back of the ladle to smooth it out thinly.
4. As the pancake cooks, add a few more drops of oil, lifting the edge of the pancake to let the oil go under. Flip when the bottom is golden, and cook until both sides are done.
5. Repeat with the remaining batter.

Nutrition (per serving)
Calories 99, fat 4 g, carbs 11 g, sugar 0 g,
Protein 2 g, sodium 175 mg

Dosa Pancakes

Dosas are a flavorful Indian crepe that is often used as a kind of wrap. These ones are served with a fried egg, but you can enjoy customizing this nutritious dish with your favorite ingredients.

Serves 4 | Prep. time 15 minutes | Cooking time 25 minutes

Ingredients
1 tablespoon rapeseed oil
1 teaspoon mustard seeds
¼ cup chickpea flour
½ cup all-purpose flour
1¼ cups skim milk
Salt and pepper to taste
Oil for frying
4 eggs, fried
3 tablespoons freshly chopped cilantro
Sliced red chili

Directions
1. In an 8-inch nonstick frying pan, heat the oil.
2. Add the mustard seeds to the oil and cook for 2 to 3 minutes, until they start to pop. Set them aside.
3. In a large mixing bowl, combine the chickpea flour, all-purpose flour, and milk. Season with salt and pepper to taste. Gently whisk to form a smooth batter.
4. Warm some oil in a nonstick frying pan over medium heat.
5. Pour some of the pancake mixture into the warm pan and cook the thin pancakes for about 2 minutes on each side.
6. When the crepes are done, serve them with a fried egg, some freshly chopped cilantro, and slices of red chili.

Nutrition (per serving)
Calories 206, fat 6 g, carbs 23 g, sugar 1 g,
Protein 12 g, sodium 65 mg

Fluffy American Pancakes with Bacon and Avocado

Here's a way you can turn your favorite pancakes into a meal, complete with bacon.

Serves 4 | Prep. time 20 minutes | Cooking time 10 minutes

Ingredients

For the pancakes
¾ cup self-rising flour
½ teaspoon cream of tartar
1 tablespoon granulated sugar
2 large eggs, room temperature
1¼ cups whole milk

For serving
10 strips of bacon, fried until crispy
2–3 tablespoons butter
2 avocados, sliced and coated with lime juice
7 ounces feta cheese
2–3 tablespoons maple syrup

Directions

1. To make the pancake batter, mix the flour, cream of tartar, sugar, eggs, and milk together in a bowl.
2. Warm the oil in a nonstick frying pan over medium heat and spoon in the pancake batter a ¼ cup at a time. Cook on each side for about 3 minutes.
3. Serve the pancakes with fried bacon, butter, sliced avocado, and feta cheese.
4. Drizzle everything with a little bit of maple syrup.

Nutrition (per serving)

Calories 572, fat 41 g, carbs 42 g, sugar 15 g,
Protein 17 g, sodium 668 mg

Sweetcorn Pancakes with Smoked Salmon Lemon Ricotta Spinach Filling

This dish has a complex flavor profile that is sure to make an impression.

Serves 4 | Prep. time 20 minutes | Cooking time 30 minutes

Ingredients
1¾ cups all-purpose flour
Pinch of salt
2 large eggs, room temperature
2 cups whole milk
7 ounces baby spinach
1 cup ricotta cheese
Juice of 1 lemon
Salt and pepper to taste
2 corn cobs
2 tablespoons butter
7 ounces smoked salmon
Fresh dill, for serving

Directions
1. In a large mixing bowl, combine the flour and salt. Make an indent in the center.
2. In the center, add the eggs and mix, and then incorporate the milk and mix them into the flour.
3. Dip the spinach into boiling water for a few seconds and squeeze out any excess liquid.
4. Mix the spinach, ricotta cheese, and lemon juice with salt and pepper to taste and set aside.
5. In a pot with boiling water, boil the corn cobs for 5 minutes. Drain, and separate the kernels from the cob. Stir them into the pancake batter.
6. Warm the butter in a nonstick frying pan over medium heat and add the pancake batter, a few tablespoons at a time.
7. Cook for 2–3 minutes on each side, or until golden brown in color. Repeat with the rest of the batter.

8. Serve 2 pancakes per person, topped with the ricotta and spinach mixture and garnished with some smoked salmon.
9. To garnish, sprinkle some freshly chopped dill and enjoy.

Nutrition (per serving)
Calories 547, fat 20 g, carbs 60 g, sugar 8 g,
Protein 31 g, sodium 1278 mg

Creamy Smoked Haddock and Prawn Crepes

These crepes filled with rich, creamy smoked haddock sauce are a crowd pleaser for seafood lovers.

Serves 4 | Prep. time 10 minutes | Cooking time 20 minutes

Ingredients
For the pancakes
1 cup all-purpose flour
1 large egg, room temperature
1¼ cup whole milk
Butter for frying

For the filling
1 tablespoon butter
2 tablespoons all-purpose flour
¾ cup whole milk
10 ounces smoked haddock fillet, flaked
1 teaspoon Dijon mustard
Juice of 1 lemon
2 cups prawns, cooked and peeled
A handful of chopped fresh dill

Directions
1. In a large mixing bowl, combine the flour, egg, and whole milk. Mix until smooth.
2. Warm the butter in a nonstick frying pan over medium heat and add some of the crepe batter.
3. Swirl the pan to spread the batter evenly.
4. Cook for about 2 minutes or until golden brown. Flip to cook the other side. Repeat with the rest of the batter, setting the cooked crepes on a plate covered with a damp paper towel to keep them warm.
5. Make the filling. In a large pan over medium heat, melt the butter and stir in the flour. Cook for about 2 minutes.
6. Gradually whisk in the whole milk and cook, stirring constantly, until the mixture thickens.
7. Stir in the flaked smoked haddock, Dijon mustard, and lemon juice.

8. Fold in the cooked prawns and freshly chopped dill and mix until everything is combined and heated through.
9. Spread some of the sauce on each crepe, fold, and serve.

Nutrition (per serving)
Calories 322, fat 7 g, carbs 28 g, sugar 4 g,
Protein 33 g, sodium 250 mg

Creamy Chicken and Mushroom Crespelles

Crespelle is Italy's version of crepes, and they're just as versatile and delicious! Try this recipe filled with chicken, mushrooms, and herbs.

Serves 4 | Prep. time 20 minutes | Cooking time 30 minutes

Ingredients
2 cups all-purpose flour
Pinch of salt
2 large eggs, room temperature
2 cups whole milk
Butter for frying

For the filling
2 tablespoons olive oil
3 shallots, finely chopped
2 garlic cloves, minced
5 fresh thyme sprigs
1 pound chicken breasts, cooked and diced to ½ inch cubes
7 ounces button mushrooms, diced
2 tablespoons butter
2 tablespoons flour
1½ cups whole milk

Vegetable oil, for frying

Directions
1. Preheat the oven to 350°F (177°C) and butter a baking dish.
2. Prepare the chicken mixture. In a large pan over medium heat, warm the olive oil and cook the shallots and garlic for 5 minutes, until soft and translucent.
3. Add the thyme and the diced chicken pieces and mushrooms. Turn up the heat and toss until browned. Transfer the mixture to a heatproof bowl.
4. In a saucepan over medium heat melt the butter and cook the flour for a minute or so.

5. Slowly pour the whole milk whisking until creamy and delicious. Set it aside.
6. To make the crespelle batter, in a large mixing bowl, combine the flour, salt, eggs, and whole milk. Mix until combined.
7. Warm the butter in a nonstick frying pan over medium heat and spoon in enough batter just to cover the bottom. Cook on each side for about 3 minutes.
8. Transfer the crespelle to a work surface and spoon some of the chicken mixture on the center.
9. Arrange the crespelles in the baking dish and pour the sauce on top. Bake for 15 minutes.

Nutrition (per serving)
Calories 615, fat 24 g, carbs 59 g, sugar 13 g,
Protein 42 g, sodium 307 mg

Cream Cheese and Herbs Pancakes

Upgrade your breakfast with a few surprisingly simple additions. Feel free to change the herbs to suit your liking!

Serves 4–6 | Prep. time 10 minutes | Cooking time 10 minutes

Ingredients
1½ cups all-purpose flour
Pinch of salt
1½ teaspoons baking powder
2¼ cups buttermilk
2 tablespoons cream cheese, softened
2 large eggs, room temperature
2 tablespoons butter, melted
1 tablespoon freshly chopped parsley
1 tablespoon freshly chopped dill
1 tablespoon freshly chopped chives
1 tablespoon freshly chopped basil
Cream cheese and extra herbs, for serving

Directions
1. In a large mixing bowl, mix the flour, salt, and baking powder.
2. Add the buttermilk, cream cheese, and eggs and mix to combine.
3. Stir in the melted butter, chopped parsley, dill, chives, and basil.
4. Warm a nonstick frying pan over medium heat and spray it with cooking spray or brush it with a little bit of butter to prevent your pancakes from sticking.
5. Scoop the batter into the hot pan using a ¼ cup measure. Cook for 2–3 minutes and flip the pancake. Cook for 2 more minutes on this side.
6. Serve your pancakes garnished with a little more cream cheese and chopped herbs.

Nutrition (per serving)
Calories 275, fat 14 g, carbs 29 g, sugar 5 g,
Protein 6 g, sodium 139 mg

Spring Onion and Sour Cream Pancakes

Sour cream and mild onion are a favorite flavor combo the whole world over. Your family or guests will love these simple pancakes as a brunch or side dish.

Serves 4–6 | Prep. time 10 minutes | Cooking time 10 minutes

Ingredients
1½ cups all-purpose flour
Pinch of salt
1½ teaspoons baking powder
2¼ cups whole milk
2 large eggs, room temperature
¼ cup sour cream
2 tablespoons butter, melted
2 spring onions, chopped
Sour cream and chopped spring onion, to serve

Directions
1. In a large mixing bowl, combine the flour, salt, and baking powder.
2. Add the milk, eggs, and sour cream.
3. Mix until combined and stir in the melted butter and spring onion.
4. Warm a nonstick frying pan over medium heat and spray it with cooking spray or brush it with a little bit of butter to prevent your pancakes from sticking.
5. Cook for 2–3 minutes and flip. Cook for 2 more minutes.
6. Serve your pancakes with some extra sour cream and diced spring onion on top.

Nutrition (per serving)
Calories 300, fat 13 g, carbs 35 g, sugar 6 g,
Protein 10 g, sodium 145 mg

Maple Bacon Pancakes

The whole family will rush to the table when they smell these delicious pancakes cooking! Here's a perfect side dish to go with your scrambled eggs.

Serves 4–6 | Prep. time 10 minutes | Cooking time 10 minutes

Ingredients
1½ cups all-purpose flour
Pinch of salt
1½ teaspoons baking soda
2¼ cups whole milk
2 large eggs, room temperature
2 tablespoons butter, melted
7 strips bacon, cooked and chopped
¼ cup maple syrup

Directions
1. In a large mixing bowl, combine the flour, salt, and baking powder.
2. Gently stir in whole milk, eggs, and melted butter.
3. Stir in the melted butter and chopped bacon.
4. Warm a nonstick frying pan over medium heat and spray it with cooking spray or brush it with a little bit of butter to prevent your pancakes from sticking.
5. Cook for 2–3 minutes, until bubbles form on the surface, and then flip them over. Cook another minute on the other side.
6. Serve with a drizzle of maple syrup.

Nutrition (per serving)
Calories 457, fat 21 g, carbs 44 g, sugar 15 g,
Protein 19 g, sodium 1130 mg

Asparagus Crespelle

Serves 6 | Prep. time 20 minutes | Cooking time 45 minutes

Ingredients
20 ounces fresh asparagus, trimmed
3 tablespoons, olive oil
¾ cup all-purpose flour
1 cup whole milk
2 large eggs, room temperature
2 tablespoons grated Parmesan cheese
Salt and pepper to taste
2 cups bechamel sauce
1 cup grated Gruyere cheese

Directions
1. Preheat the oven to 400°F (204°C) and butter a roasting pan and a baking dish.
2. Arrange the asparagus on the pan and drizzle with olive oil. Roast for 20 minutes.
3. Meanwhile, in a large mixing bowl, combine the flour, milk, and eggs until smooth.
4. Warm the oil in a nonstick frying pan and add some of the crepe batter. Swirl the pan to make a thin crepe.
5. Cook the crepes for about 2 minutes on each side. Repeat the same process with the rest of the batter.
6. When the asparagus comes out of the oven, sprinkle it with grated Parmesan cheese and season with salt and pepper to taste.
7. Reduce the oven temperature to 350°F (177°C).
8. Fill the crepes with baked asparagus and half of the bechamel sauce. Roll the crepes and arrange them in the prepared baking dish.
9. Spread the remaining bechamel sauce on top and add the grated Gruyere.
10. Bake for another 15 minutes.

Nutrition (per serving)
Calories 352, fat 20 g, carbs 25 g, sugar 7 g,
Protein 18 g, sodium 540 mg

Mini Pancake Canapes

Serves 4–6 | Prep. time 15 minutes | Cooking time 10 minutes

Ingredients
1½ cups all-purpose flour
Pinch of salt
1½ teaspoons baking powder
1 cup whole milk
1¼ cups sparkling water
2 tablespoons butter, melted
2 large eggs, room temperature
7 ounces cream cheese, softened
1 tablespoon freshly chopped parsley
1 tablespoon freshly chopped dill
1 tablespoon freshly chopped chives
1 tablespoon freshly chopped basil
Salt and pepper to taste

Directions
1. In a large mixing bowl, combine the flour, salt, and baking powder.
2. Gently mix in the milk, sparkling water, melted butter, and eggs.
3. Warm a nonstick frying pan over medium heat and spray it with cooking spray or brush it with a little bit of butter to prevent your pancakes from sticking.
4. Add 2 tablespoons of batter at a time to the pan to form the canapes. Cook for 1–2 minutes, until golden, and then flip them over to finish cooking.
5. Meanwhile, in a medium mixing bowl, combine the cream cheese with the herbs, salt, and pepper. Transfer the mixture to a piping bag with a large star tip. Keep the mixture chilled until ready to use.
6. Let the canapes cool, and then pipe swirls of herbed cream cheese on top. Serve immediately.

Nutrition (per serving)
Calories 377, fat 22 g, carbs 33 g, sugar 2 g,
Protein 11 g, sodium 233 mg

RECIPE INDEX

APPENDIX

Cooking Conversion Charts

1. Measuring Equivalent Chart

Type	Imperial	Imperial	Metric
Weight	1 dry ounce		28g
	1 pound	16 dry ounces	0.45 kg
Volume	1 teaspoon		5 ml
	1 dessert spoon	2 teaspoons	10 ml
	1 tablespoon	3 teaspoons	15 ml
	1 Australian tablespoon	4 teaspoons	20 ml
	1 fluid ounce	2 tablespoons	30 ml
	1 cup	16 tablespoons	240 ml
	1 cup	8 fluid ounces	240 ml
	1 pint	2 cups	470 ml
	1 quart	2 pints	0.95 l
	1 gallon	4 quarts	3.8 l
Length	1 inch		2.54 cm

Numbers are rounded to the closest equivalent

2. Oven Temperature Equivalent Chart

Fahrenheit (°F)	Celsius (°C)	Gas Mark
220	100	
225	110	1/4
250	120	½
275	140	1
300	150	2
325	160	3
350	180	4
375	190	5
400	200	6
425	220	7
450	230	8
475	250	9
500	260	

*   Celsius (°C) = T (°F)-32] * 5/9
** Fahrenheit (°F) = T (°C) * 9/5 + 32
*** Numbers are rounded to the closest equivalent

Manufactured by Amazon.ca
Bolton, ON

40365800R00048